How to Break into a Computer Career through Self-Study!

How to Break into a Computer Career through Self-Study!

Tom Graves

Writers Club Press
San Jose New York Lincoln Shanghai

How to Break into a Computer Career through Self-Study!

Writers Club Press
an imprint of iUniverse, Inc.

For information address:
iUniverse, Inc.
5220 S 16th, Ste. 200
Lincoln, NE 68512
www.iuniverse.com

ISBN: 0-595-20036-2

Printed in the United States of America

Dedication

This is dedicated to all of the people out there who want a better life but haven't quite realized how to do it.

CONTENTS

PREFACE

A few short years ago I knew absolutely nothing about computers. My roommate in the U.S. Coast Guard bought a computer and in order for me to use it he had to write directions so that I could start a chess game he had. When I got out of the Coast Guard I didn't have much money but I did have some time. This was even though I was working and going to College full-time.

When I got my first computer job I found that very little of what I had studied in school was of any use. Instead I found that the articles I had read in magazines and the computer books I had read from the bookstore were more useful on the job.

Today in my current work almost everything I do I learned from the books I bought at a bookstore and not from College classes. I like going to College and learning new things, but in the job market I've found that technology changes too fast and schools couldn't seem to catch up.

This book is the advice I wish I'd had back when I got out of the Coast Guard. There was no one to make suggestions as to what course I should take in starting my career. I think I could have saved a lot of time if I had known what to study to begin with.

ACKNOWLEDGEMENTS

So many people have helped me over these last few years. First, I would like to thank my wife, **Ewa**, for taking a chance on marrying a poor student who just got out of the Coast Guard. Next I would like to thank **Mike Bowman** for teaching me so many things about computers when we worked together at Davidson & Assoc. I would also like to thank **John Robinson** for giving me my first programming job, my **Dad** for buying my first computer when neither of us had any money, **Lt. Guy T. Pilla, USCG**, who encouraged me with my education and was a good job reference, **Dennis Victor** for giving me the idea to write this book, and everyone who ever answered one of my questions on computers. A person cannot really survive in this world alone.

INTRODUCTION

This book is intended for two types of people. The first is a person who wants to change careers. Maybe that person is an actor who has been waiting tables for twenty years, and as they get older find that that big break may not be coming their way. They still want to act, but at the same time would like to get a better paying job while they wait.

Another person may just be tired with what they are doing and want to do something else. They also don't have the money for a Technical School or four years to go to College full-time. College is a good place to start but not everybody has the desire or the time to study for such a long time.

The second type of person is someone who has finished College but finds that they don't have the knowledge to work in a cutting edge area of computing. In this case some self-study is essential.

Maybe one of these people will also find that studying in the privacy of his or her home and at his or her own speed, they are able to learn a lot more. I am one of these people. My emphasis in studying something is to understand it. Not to pass some exam so I can get a certificate. When you take the time to learn something well and really understand it you are ahead of many people. You will actually be competent at your job and because of that you will be more valuable than gold to your employer. The reason for this, sadly enough, is because competence in the workplace seems to be rather rare. Part of this competence is caring about your job. That is something only you can supply. But if you like your type of work, and in this case, computers, you already have this taken care of.

When you are thinking about changing careers you have a couple of options open to you. One of them is to go to College and get a degree in the field you're interested in. This is a good idea if you can. College degrees are good for getting your foot into higher paying jobs and maybe advancing in your career. But four years (full-time) is a long and hard time when you still have to work full-time and maybe even have a family to take care of.

Not having a College degree shouldn't stop you from getting into a computer career. You may have heard of the many stories of someone with no or little college doing great in a computer career.

The key requirement for many employers is competence. Can you do a good job? After that they will look at your education and experience. This isn't every employer of course, and I'm sure in your job search you'll find many exceptions. But many computer jobs go unfilled or take a long time to fill. These jobs are what you will be after.

If you have the desire to change your life then you can do it! What better way to spend your spare time than to improve your life? Think about your future and start on the road towards that. If you just don't give up, if you don't listen to all the reasons the world will give you for giving up, then you will eventually reach your goals.

GO FOR IT!

CHAPTER 1

WELCOME TO THE REST OF YOUR LIFE!

Welcome to the beginning of the rest of your life. That's kind of a cliché but definitely true. So you want to break into a computer career, eh? I don't mean slide in; I don't mean squeeze into the computer industry. I mean to break in! And by that I mean to change careers or to start a new career without going back to college, or even going to college at all.

Maybe you don't have a degree and you don't have the time to get a degree. Maybe you don't want to spend four or more years going to school. You may have thought of going to a technical school but some of them are $10,000 or more for only a few weeks or months of training. You could get a Student loan but if you're like me you don't like the idea of being so heavily in debt. The only alternative and a very good and inexpensive one is to teach yourself through self-study. This would only require a few easily obtainable books about computers, a computer or two, and the discipline to finish what you start. If this sounds like you, then you're holding the right book.

This book is intended for the person that finds they need to get skills, which employers need, so as to create a career in the computer field. This is the least expensive way and possibly the best way to learn computers. Some people aren't comfortable with this approach. They want the discipline that a class would impose on them and they like to have a teacher handy to answer questions. Having a teacher around is quite convenient. But you still need to read the book yourself, and the teacher isn't usually around to answer questions when you are at home. There are other ways to get help, especially now that the Internet has become so popular.

Let's say that you want to write programs for a living. A school will usually give you an introduction to the overall world of computers, but they often don't teach you what happens in the real world. The problem colleges have is that the teachers often have not been in the real world for many years, and so are stuck in what **used** to be state-of-the-art computer science. Things change very fast in the computer business. Schools have traditionally had a problem with this.

I admit I have a degree. I have a Master's degree in Software Engineering. But I had a career in Networking before my days in College, and not one employer seemed to care about me going to school.

In my current job everything that I do with the exception of some databases I design I learned on my own from books. I studied book, after book, after book, and played with the latest technologies on my computer at home. The latest technologies are what are really wanted in the job market.

Your life is your own game. You can sit in your living room and watch television or you can do something that will get you closer to your goals. No one else will do it for you. If you want to take your life into your own hands then read on.

Now, this book is not intended to teach you everything you need to know about computers. What this book is going to do is to introduce you to the different paths you could take in a computer career, and teach you just enough about these different areas so that you can make an informed decision about what further study you should take. This is only going to get you started. You will still need to do all of the studying on your own.

When I started out learning computers I had nobody to tell me anything. I didn't have anybody to ask questions about what to study. I didn't have anybody to help me when I didn't understand something or tell me where to look for the answers. I had to do all these things on my own. This was long before I got a Masters degree in Software Engineering. And in fact the Masters degree didn't really answer too many questions anyway.

The person that might find this information useful is someone who is basically in the same position I was in a few years ago. You may have just gotten out of the military, as I did, or you may find yourself in a Security Guard job that is getting you nowhere (as I did), or you just may be enticed by the rumors you hear of all the money that people make. You may also not have a lot of money to spend on training schools. In that case self-study is a good choice.

If you are in college now or you have just gotten your degree then this information is still for you. But you don't **need** a college degree to break into a computer career. There is plenty of room for people who start the non-traditional way. And by non-traditional I mean to study books on your own, experiment on your own, and do everything yourself. You will take complete responsibility for your own training, career, and life.

Whether you go to a training school, college, or study on your own, it all boils down to the same thing: You must learn the information you're studying. It sounds so obvious that it seems ridiculous I'm telling you this. But I have known students that endlessly blame a teacher or a book for their inability to learn the material. It is true that a teacher can be exceptionally boring, but you still have the textbook, so never mind the teacher. If the book you have is bad, return it and get another one. Read more than one book on a subject and you will gain an even better understanding of the subject no matter how much you learned from the first book.

If you are in a boring job or a dead end career the computer field may just be for you. But to get to a point where someone will pay you to play with computers you will need to spend a great deal of your personal time studying and experimenting. Are you willing to do this? Are you willing to skip going out to clubs in order to stay at home and study? Or if you don't go to clubs but instead only have that couple hours at night to spare after the kids have gone to sleep; are you willing to spend that time studying for possibly several months or even a couple of years?

You can learn everything you need to know to have a good career in computers just from books that you read at home. I did it and it takes a lot of work. But I was tired of being poor. When I did work as a Security Guard I had time to do things but no money. When I worked two jobs I had the money but no time. So I decided to get paid more for less work. That sounds ideal doesn't it? But the only way to do this is to gain knowledge and be able to do things others can't. Remember that old law of supply and demand. If fewer people can do something then those that can are more valuable. Coconuts fall off the trees and can just be picked up in the South Pacific. But in California you pay a couple of dollars for one. So instead of being that free coconut in Samoa, you want to be that $2.00 coconut in California.

As for the big money you hear about, some of it is true, but some of it is just hype (exaggeration). To a business the bottom line (profit) is the only thing that matters. So they will try to get you for as little as they can. That doesn't mean that you won't be offered that great money you hear about. It just means that the people who get that great money already have experience and are probably senior people. With this book, and continued study after you have a job, you will be on your way to the career you've dreamed of.

When I say *continued* study, I mean it. I had a boss who was rather dissatisfied with some of the people that were working for him because they were content with their positions and didn't want to put out any extra effort. If you are content with your job and never want to advance that is up to you. Each person wants something different in life. But even if you want to stay in the same position you are in, you won't be able to just stay there. This is because computer technology is always changing. Even if you want to stay where you are you will still need to study to keep up to date. That is another commitment you will need to make if you decide on a computer career.

After you have gained this knowledge in an unorthodox manner (as in just self-study and without college) then comes the task of convincing an employer that you know what you're talking about. That's something different. This is something even people who went to college need to do. Though it's harder to do when you don't have a degree.

Some people think the Internet is something for complete geeks who cannot socialize with people and have nothing better to do with their time than sit in a darkened room and eat Twinkies. But the Internet is your window to the world. In this course of self-study that you have chosen this will be an invaluable resource for finding answers to questions and connecting up with people who may be able to help you. The Internet is also especially good if you end up at a job where there are no other computer people, and you have no one to ask questions. This has happened to me on two jobs as a Network Administrator and as a Programmer. At a small company you may be the entire Information Technology department.

There are three areas in the computer industry that you can get into and make a living at. One of these is Networking. The other is Software Design and the third is Web Development. While all of these can be learned from books at home they often have different requirements for getting into.

The job I have now is writing business programs in Visual Basic at a large company. But most of the knowledge I use in my day-to-day job did not come from college. It came from books that I spent time reading at home, experimenting with the material in the book on my computer, and making it work even when it doesn't seem to want to.

The whole object of reading anything is to understand it. You do not read something and then walk away without understanding the contents. If that was so then what was the point of reading the book to begin with? There are a lot of new words in every job and area of study. Finding out what these words mean is part of learning the new subject. Don't try and cheat on this step. Not only will you not understand what you're reading, but also someday you will make a big mistake because of it, or you'll get caught and look like a fool. When you're starting out in a new career you want to do everything you can to make your employer and customers confident in your abilities. The first step in this is to know the terminology in your area of expertise.

Every book you are reading you are reading because you want to learn something new. If that weren't true you wouldn't be reading the book. So, what is important is what knowledge you walk away from that book with. It doesn't matter how fast you read, or how many questions you ask someone, or even how many times you read the book. What matters is what knowledge you gain from your reading.

I once had a math teacher who told a story about one of his students. This student took Elementary Algebra three times. He failed the first two, but passed the third time. He then went on to fail Intermediate Algebra once or twice and finally passed it the second time. He went on this way, failing class after class, but never stopping until he finally passed it. Eventually he got his Ph.D. in mathematics. Some might call this student slow. Others might call him dumb. It doesn't matter what anyone called him, in the end he still got his Ph.D.

Maybe someone else earned his or her Ph.D. in three or four years. Maybe it took this slow student eight years. But in the end they both had the same knowledge. For some people it is harder to learn. If you are one of them, so what. It may be harder for you but you can still do it, and have the same knowledge as someone who is faster. In the end you will have the same knowledge as a faster student and maybe you'll know the material better because you looked at it longer. So you need to understand what it is you're reading because that's the idea, otherwise it's just a waste of time, and you might as well be doing something for fun.

Breaking into this business through self-study requires effort and discipline. Of course you are free to follow the traditional path towards a computer career, but I am assuming that you are not, and that's why you have this book. You are going to keep a job because you know computers. You are going to be worth *every* penny they pay you because you won't be relying on a diploma from some university that *says* you know what you're talking about. You actually *will* know what you're talking about.

You may get the impression that I don't feel going to college is a good thing. But what I really mean is that too often just by attending class and turning in some term paper a teacher will feel that you understand the subject. But as is too often the case this is not true. Just because you heard what the teacher said and can repeat it back to them does not mean that you *understand* what they said. But it also does not mean that you don't understand the subject either. You may know every word that the teacher said and be able to apply everything. What I am saying is that if you *know* computers, if you *know* software, if you *know* whatever it is you are doing, you will be able to find a job and keep it.

One last thing I want to mention is the value and difference between studying at home and paying for a technical school. I will admit that I have done most of my studying at home. I have a bias towards studying at home. I find that if you are able to read things, and you are able to figure out how they work by yourself (with some help of course), it will then be easier for you later in your career to learn new things. The computer business is constantly changing and even when you get your first job you will need to study new things as the industry and computers change.

Many people feel that they need a teacher to ask questions if they get into trouble. This is a valid reason to take a class somewhere. But some technical schools charge an outrageous fee to teach you things. What happens when you take the class? You listen to a teacher tell you what is in the textbook that is sitting in front you. You still need to learn the material yourself. Whether you get the knowledge from a book or a teacher you are the one that still has to learn the material.

It's true that if you have difficulty you can ask a teacher about the problem. And that may be worth the fee that you pay. But there is a lot of help on the Internet and in other places. I'm not saying that it will always be easy to get an answer to a question on the Internet (Many times you may need to call someone at a software company or even the author of a book to get the answer). It's just that you have to balance how much you're paying for the service that you're receiving.

When I decided to get into computers I did not have a lot of money. So the choice was made for me. The choice is yours to decide as your situation dictates. But I would suggest doing as much as possible at home on your own computer.

And I would recommend buying your own computer if you don't already have one. Computers do not cost a lot of money these days, and I would definitely suggest buying your own even if you do not have a lot of money. Think of it as an investment in your future. I had a friend once that said she would never hire anybody to work with computers who did not own a computer themselves. This view may not be justified but it's much easier to experiment with things yourself at home, on your own computer, than it is to try to either borrow one or to use a school's computer laboratory. And you don't need the latest and greatest computer that is on the market. You can buy an old used one for next to nothing from the classified ads in the local newspaper.

For every dollar you spend buying a piece of software, a computer, or a book, think of it as an investment in your future. For every minute you spend actually learning something from a book, think of it as investment in the future.

By the way, I would recommend buying a computer that runs a version of the Microsoft Windows Operating System. These include Windows 95, Windows 98, Windows 2000, and Window NT (New Technology). I'm not saying this because I don't like other types of computers such as Macintosh or UNIX computers. I'm saying this because from what I have seen and heard most businesses use Windows operating system computers and this is what you should practice on. If later in this book you decide you want to use the UNIX operating system you can easily put a version of UNIX called LINUX on the Windows computer. You cannot, however, switch over to a Macintosh if you decide you want it later. You'll have to buy a completely different computer.

Remember that old Chinese saying, "A journey of a thousand miles begins with a single step". By buying this book you have taken that first step. Just keep on going and don't stop along the way and eventually you'll get to that dream of yours.

CHAPTER 2

I JUST BOUGHT A COMPUTER, NOW WHAT?

If you've just bought a computer, or you have no idea what to do with the one you have, then you should first get a book on computer basics.

A book that looks good is "SAMS Teach Yourself Computer Basics in 24 Hours".

There are several other books at your local bookstore or at an online bookstore that will get you familiar with the basic operation of a computer. I like the short chapters in SAMS "24 Hour" books and the "21 Day" books. I think it allows you to feel like you've accomplished something each time you finish a chapter, and it teaches a little section of the subject with each "day" or "hour".

CHAPTER 3

WHAT AREA DO I SPECIALIZE IN?

There are three areas that you can specialize in. You really need to specialize in one area rather than try to learn everything about computers. The reason for this is that employers will be looking for a "network person", or a "Software Designer", or a "Web Master". They will not be looking for just a COMPUTER person. While all of these people work in computers and have a lot of functions that overlap, if you were a software designer you won't be receiving telephone calls from users who want you to fix the colors on their computer screen. That would be what a Network Person would be doing.

So, you need to decide what area you want to concentrate your effort in. This will also do you the service of concentrating your time in one area so that you can be an expert in that area instead of a jack-of-all-trades. When somebody hires you to do a job they want you to be an expert. Even if they hire you for an entry-level position and don't really expect you to know too much, if you know more than everybody else does that is applying for the job, you will get hired.

The three general areas that you can specialize in are *Web Development*, *Network Administration*, and *Software Development*.

Web Development is where you create Web sites on the Internet or for a private Internet for a company. A private Internet is called an "Intranet".

If you have been on the Internet and looked at Web pages then this is the kind of thing that you would be creating as a Web Developer. If you've never been on the Internet and you've never seen a web page then you may want to check out the Internet and see what this is all about.

The second area is Network Administration. This is the area where you would be taking care of a computer network for a company. Just in case you don't know, a network is nothing more can a bunch of computers connected to each other and thus able to communicate. Most companies have a network to share resources between their different computers. For instance, without a network you would need to buy one printer (a resource) for every computer in your company. With a network you can buy one printer and have everybody share it. So companies usually connect all of their personal computers together and share printers as well as other functions you'll learn about later.

But when you are doing network administration, you are not just taking care of the network and the connections. You also will get many telephone calls about the average everyday problems that your Users will be having with their personal computers (in a business, personal computers are usually called Work Stations).

So, in the Network Administration area of the computer industry, you will be dealing a lot with all the people in your company who are using computers on a day-to-day basis. This will be everything from dealing with the connections from your company in California to another company in Australia, to helping a user figure out how to format a disc, or even how to start a program on their Workstation. This job will often include fixing the hardware on the Workstations as well.

The third area that you can specialize in is Software Development (programming and the design of the software). This is what many people think about when they think of computers. The person who tells the computer what to do in the software that you might buy at a store. This is the area that you use a computer language to translate your thoughts into instructions that the computer will follow to do a job. Anytime that you have used electronic mail, or even played a CD on your computer, there has been a program telling the computer what to do. You can tell the computer to do just about anything you want it to do. But a computer is not an intelligent machine. It only does exactly what you tell it to do. If the computer makes a mistake, then it was the programmers' fault. Fault is not really a good word to use, what I really mean to say is that if a computer makes a mistake then it was a mistake the programmer told it to do. The programmer did not mean to tell it to make that mistake but nonetheless he or she did.

Of the three areas I have mentioned, this is the one area that having a degree from a University may be of some use. But it would be mostly useful in getting your first job, not because you would learn anymore than you would be studying books at home. But, it is still not a requirement. There are many companies that are in dire need of programmers and if you can just demonstrate that you actually know how to write programs then they may be willing to hire you into an entry-level position.

My first degree was in English. And I thought just having a degree would help me find a job. But I did not have a degree in computer science and so I had a difficult time getting interviews for programming positions. But that again depends on what languages you know, and how needed your skills are to companies at that time.

Again, remember that everything that I say is only true from my experience. You may find that things are different where you are or at the time that you start looking for a job. I can't say whether or not large old companies such as IBM, QUALCOMM, etc. like to see, if not actually require, a degree from people they hire. But I used to work for a large, older company where there were only two people doing what I did in the client/server group. The one other person did not have a degree, and yet he knew more than most college graduates know about writing programs. That company would not offer him a full-time regular position until he had his degree. So he was being an intern, and when he got his degree they would offer him a regular full-time position as a software developer. In this case having a degree would have been useful, but only because the Human Resources department wanted everybody to have a college degree, not because he knew more than anybody else did.

CHAPTER 4

WEB DEVELOPMENT

Web Development is relatively new to the world. But this may also be where you may make good money, and it will probably be easier to get into this area of the computer business than into Software Development.

Web Development is where you write what a person would see when they "surf" the Internet. Now the Internet is actually a worldwide network of computers. When you use your PC at home and you connect to the Internet you can go to certain computers in the world and request to see their "Web pages". Web pages are basically documents that somebody has put onto these computers, to allow people to get information, order a product, or see something else like that.

Web Pages range anywhere from completely useful information like the specifications for a dish washing machine, all the way to totally useless information like the biography of your favorite television star. It's actually a very useful way to the communicate information to the entire world. It does not require approval from any government, nor anybody else; it is just free speech across the world. (There are some countries, though, that attempt to restrict the information displayed in their countries by filtering all web page requests through a central government office).

There is a good possibility that you have already "surfed" the Web and that is why you are interested in the computer business. If you already are familiar with the Web then what I am about to say may seem very elementary. And of course you won't need the following section, "How to use a Browser". But as I said, I am assuming that somebody reading this book knows nothing about computers and I will try to make things as simple as possible, and explain everything I can.

The reason that I am starting this chapter out with instructions on how to use a browser is that if you are considering a career in Web Development you need to first take a look at what your product should look like.

How To Use A Browser

The way that you get onto the Internet is first, of course, to have a personal computer. On your Personal Computer is a program called a "Browser" that would enable you to see these "Web Pages". There are a number of free browsers available on the Internet; the two most popular are Internet Explorer by Microsoft and Netscape Navigator by Netscape. By the way don't let the disagreement that you may hear over which browser is better confuse you. Both browsers are very good and the only real difference is personal opinion.

Your personal computer may already have a browser installed when you buy it. If it doesn't then all you need to do is call an ISP (Internet Service Provider) and ask for their CD with software on it. It will then be sent to you in the mail. An Internet Service Provider is a company where you would use your telephone line, and dial into the ISP's computers and thus connect to the Internet. Some famous examples of this are MSN (Microsoft Network), CompuServe, and AOL (America Online). You can contact MSN at 1-800-373-3676, CompuServe at 1-800-848-8990 and AOL at 1-800-827-6364.

A newer computer will probably have these ISPs already on them and just waiting for you to start their service. But if not, call the above numbers.

One thing I have not talked about yet is that you will need something called a modem to connect to the Internet. Just about all computers you buy now already have a modem in them. I'll explain about this later but for now just realize that the computer you buy must have a modem in it, or you must get one installed.

So, now that you are connected to the Internet you need to tell your Browser which computer on the Internet you want to connect to. Each Web Site on the Internet, and by Web Site I mean a location on the Internet that has Web Pages, has an address just as any location in a city has an address. What you are in fact telling the browser is where on the Internet you want to get the Web pages. This address is also called a URL or Uniform Resource Locator. You will hear URL used quite a bit in "Web Speak".

You would type the URL in the space at the top of the browser that probably says "http://". A URL looks something like this: "www.coffee.com". The "www" part means World Wide Web. This is just another name for the Internet. The "com" part just means that this web site is a commercial web site, which means that this site belongs to a business. Other endings that you might see would be ". gov" , which means a government site, or ".mil" which would mean a military site such as "www.Navy.mil". The browser would then make your request to the web site, which would then send back to your PC the web page.

Web Development

Web development is a type of programming, but it isn't a type of programming where you use a programming language. To write Web pages you use a language called HTML, which stands for Hypertext Mark Up Language. This is not a true programming language but is actually a document formatting language. This is the same type of language that a printer would receive from a computer program telling it where to place things on the page that it's printing. We don't really need to get into that at this time, but a computer program running on your PC will send instructions to the printer as to how to print a document. And HTML is that type of language.

HTML

When HTML first started it was just a document formatting language. It just told the browser how to place text and pictures on your computer screen. So, you would write a web page using standard HTML, and just have words and pictures displayed on the screen. But now the Web has gotten much more sophisticated. Browsers allow you to do a lot more now than you used to be able to do.

JavaScript and VBScript

In addition to HTML, there are now two miniature languages that you can use to actually write small programs that will work inside of a browser. One is called JavaScript and the other is called VBScript.

These are like miniature versions of the programming language called JAVA (though it isn't actually related), and the programming language called Visual Basic. If you are going to become a Web Master and write Web pages then you will need to learn at least JavaScript. While both of these "scripting" languages are useful and do the same things, JavaScript will run in just about every browser including Netscape and Internet Explorer, while VBScript will only run in Internet Explorer.

Client Side and Server Side

On a computer that is not attached to any other computer (as it would be on a network), a program would only run on that computer. The program would then be able to do anything it wants, that your operating system would allow, and it would be able to get all of the information that it needed to perform its tasks. But when you're on the Internet there are actually two computers involved. There is the one computer that you're sitting at, which is called a "Client" machine. The computer that has the

Web pages is called a "Server" and is called a Server because it *serves* your Client machine. In other words your machine is a client of the machine serving it. By the way, when I say "machine" I mean a computer. You will find that the computer business is full of slang, and all kinds of special words that mean something other than what you are used to them meaning. This is true of all businesses, and all areas of endeavor.

So, you are sitting at the client computer and you request a web page from the server. The server then sends the web page to your browser, and your browser displays it for you. The server has absolutely no knowledge of your computer other than an "address" of where to send the web page. Your computer, the client, has no knowledge of the server except an "address" of where to request the web page from. This whole set up is called "Client/Server". The Server cannot do anything to your computer without your computer's permission. Just as you're computer cannot do anything to the Server machine without the Server's permission. So, just remember this basic setup as we go farther on in understanding what you can do with the Web and HTML.

One of the areas that this concept is important to is when you're writing a "script". A "Script" is what you would call a "program" that you write using JavaScript or VBScript. That is why JavaScript and VBScript are called "scripting" languages.

When someone writes a script it will run either on the client machine or on the server machine. In standard HTML you can write JavaScript or VBScript but it will only run on the client computer. Nothing is normally done on the server. So, you could write a normal web page that displayed pictures and words and had "links" to other Web pages, and had JavaScript or VBScript running on the client computer. And it would be a successful web page. What I have just described is what would be called *client side processing*.

So now if you look at the Internet as just another Network (networks are nothing more than two or more computers connected together and able to communicate), then you will see that you have the potential of running a program on the server or on the client. So let's say that you have a database on the Server. And the Server is in Japan. The Client computer is in Poland. Now the person in Poland is one of your salespeople and they are trying to sell Japanese cars to Polish businesses. The way the Internet is now the salesperson could connect to the Internet in Poland, through an Internet Service Provider (ISP), connect to the server in Japan through a Browser, and then update the database (a Database is just a collection of records stored in a logical manner and organized for easy retrieval) in Japan with their sales information.

Your Client computer does not have the ability to change the database on the server. The server must change it for you. This is just the natural way computers are at this time. Each machine has the ability to change itself, but it cannot change another computer without that other computer's permission. So, how does the client computer update the database on the Server?

The solution to this apparent problem is to have "script" that runs on the Server, and a script that runs on the Client computer. The browser will run the script on the client side. And the Server will run its script and do what the script tells it to do. In the case of the database update you wouldn't need a script on the client, only a script on the Server that actually updated the database. The Client would just use standard HTML to send the necessary data to the Server, and then the Server would update itself.

The Browser in Poland would send a request to the server saying to update certain records and the server in Japan that contained the database would then update the records. Of course if the person in Poland did not have permission to change those records then the Server in Japan would not change the records. It is the job of the Server computer to make sure that the person requesting the change to the records had the proper permission.

So you see, you have actions that run on the Server side of this teeter-totter and actions that run on the Client Side. Thus you get the expressions "Server Side" and "Client Side".

Once you have learned basic HTML and at least one of the scripting languages, you can go on to learn about the server side scripting that many professionals do. You could do server side scripting just in a text editor such as "Notepad" which comes with all Microsoft graphical operating systems such as Windows 98, Windows 2000 or Windows NT, or you can use software such as "Visual InterDev ", "ColdFusion", or "Net Dynamics". This software makes it easier to do scripts. Professionals often use this software and it is something you should look at after you are familiar with HTML and JavaScript.

What about things like DHTML, XML, PERL, CGI, etc?

These are advanced subjects that you might want to look at a little later.

But just so you know something about them I'll tell you a bit about each.

XML is something that is *HOT* these days. If you want to work as a Web Master or Web Designer you should learn something about it if for no other reason than it looks great on your resume. If an employer does a search of a database for all the resumes with **XML** on it, then your resume will appear. This might be how that employer sorts out whom to call in for an interview. But of course if they searched on HTML your resume would come up as well.

XML is like the brother or sister of HTML. It allows you to create your own version of a language like HTML to display things in a browser. **XML** and HTML can work together to display things the way you want them to. That is probably all you need to know until you actually get into learning it.

DHTML stands for Dynamic HTML. It is something that allows you to add movement or *User Interaction* to your web page. From what I hear it is some pretty good stuff, and games created with **DHTML** are pretty cool. The only drawback to **DHTML** is that it will only work in one of the major browsers, Internet Explorer. For those people that have Internet Explorer that will be visiting a web site you design, this will not be a problem. But to all those other people who have Netscape Navigator or another browser it will not work.

So I would not recommend learning **DHTML** in the beginning, as you want to be as marketable to prospective employers as you can be. And most employers want you to be able to write a site that is accessible to users of all browsers. That is why I recommend JavaScript and not VBScript. Personally I would prefer to use VBScript. But only Internet Explorer supports VBScript and both support JavaScript. So in the interest of getting a job, you have to think of what would make you more desirable to the greatest number of employers.

CGI was an older method of attaching a small program to a web page so that some processing of data outside of HTML could occur. This method is still used in some places especially if the web page is located on a UNIX server, but in many places this has been replaced by newer technologies such as Active Server Pages (ASP), ColdFusion, and the like. If you know the C programming language you might be interested in the book, "CGI Internet Programming with C++ and C", by Mark Felton, ISBN:0-13-712358-2.

PERL. This is a small language that is used on Web Servers and on UNIX computers. It was designed to make writing some programming tasks easier than if you had used a larger and more complex language. **PERL** is often used for **CGI** programs (or scripts), and by network administrators who are not programmers but want some task to be done that otherwise would have to be done by a program. A book that may get you started is "CGI Programming in C & PERL" by Thomas Boutell, ISBN: 0-201-42219-0.

PERL is a good thing to learn if you want to work in Web Design. There are always ten ways to do the same thing in the computer field, and you will find PERL useful in many areas on UNIX and Windows NT.

Front Page: Front Page is a software program that helps you create a web site. Much of the work can be done graphically, that is by dragging pictures and the like around the screen, etc. Many companies do seem to use this software a lot. You may even end up at one. But be aware that a true professional, while they may use this software would never depend on it to get everything done. There will be many times that you will have to dive into the HTML that Front Page creates to find out why something isn't working the way you expect it to. And the HTML that Front Page creates may not be what you are used to. As a professional, it is better if you can do it all from scratch even if you sometimes use a product like Front Page to get the bulk of the work done.

Web Server Software

On the Internet or an Intranet you can't simply put webs sites out on any computer and have it work. The Server that you put it on must be running *Web Server Software* or *Web Hosting Software.* Two of the more popular ones are *Apache Server* and Microsoft's *Internet Information Server* (also called <u>IIS</u>).

Just because I have broken this book up into three distinct career areas for you to specialize in doesn't mean that you don't have to know something about the other two areas. As you may have noticed Web Sites have a good deal of programming (software) associated with them, even though you are not writing a software product to sell to someone. This is also the case with Web Server Software. You may need to know something about how to administer the software on the server even though it has nothing to do with your web site. If you find yourself in this situation then just go to your local large bookseller and they should have something on the particular server you need to support (or try www.bn.com for tons of books that you can order online).

What Should You Do At This Point?

So now you have some idea of what the Internet is all about and what it would take to put a web page on the Internet. But what should you do now that you have decided to go into an Internet career?

Well, what I would do is to first become familiar with your computer and browser (Internet Explorer or Netscape Navigator), and surf the web for a while.

After you get the hang of how a User would see and use web sites you will be ready to learn HTML. Try a web site called www.htmlgoodies.com. This is a pretty good site, and in fact the site was turned into a book you can buy entitled, "HTML Goodies" by Joe Burns. It is published by QUE (This is a good publisher of computer books. Just about everything, if not everything from them is good). The ISBN Number is: 0-78971823-5.

This web site and book have a lot of introductory information on everything that has to do with setting up a web site including JavaScript, DHTML, and XML. Reading this book or site first would probably be a good introduction and would give you an idea of where to go at this point. The choice of what to study and in what order is your decision after all. I'm only trying to give you an idea of what I would have done if I were in your shoes.

One thing I should mention is that the web site www.htmlgoodies.com and the book use a term called a "flag". Everywhere else that I have ever seen including books, and all of the Web Masters and Web Designers I have ever talked to use the term "tag". Just remember this and don't get confused. I have emailed the author of the web site and asked him why he does this when apparently no one else does but I have only received an automated response.

Another book on HTML to consider is SAMS "Teach Yourself HTML in 21 Days".

As for books, I like the format of SAMS "21 Day" books, but there are many books out there on every computer subject, so feel free to get any book aimed at beginners.

After you read one of these books create a web site with what you have learned so that you get some practice. Think about doing a web page or site that is business related, such as a site to sell something.

Next, I would learn JavaScript. A couple of books you could try are "JavaScript: A Beginners Guide" by John Pollock. Publisher Osborne. ISBN: 0-07-213140-3, and "Teach Yourself JavaScript in 21 Days" by SAMS Publishing.

Then add some JavaScript to the web site you've already created. At this point you can probably only do Client side scripts, so take that into consideration when thinking about what kind of scripts you'll write.

Now you have the ability to create a web site that looks like one of the older style sites. But business web sites have gotten more sophisticated in the last few years. You would now want to learn Server side scripting.

You could learn Active Server Pages or ColdFusion. Both seem to be in wide use. To find out what is needed in your area you could look at the want ads in the employment section of your local newspaper, or you could possibly call a Head Hunter (Recruiter) and find out what is more often wanted in your area.

Active Server Pages are often created in Microsoft Visual InterDev (http://msdn.microsoft.com/vinterdev/default.asp). This is a program that is part of Microsoft Visual Studio. Visual Basic and Visual C++ are also part of Visual Studio. You may have heard of them, already. You can probably buy Visual InterDev separately from Visual Studio so that shouldn't be a problem. I only mention that it is part of Visual Studio because that is how Microsoft often sells it, and Software Developers buy it that way.

ColdFusion is a Server-side scripting product produced by Allaire (www.allaire.com). If you wanted to learn ColdFusion you could try the book, "SAMS Teach Yourself Allaire ColdFusion in 21 Days" by Mohnike, ISBN: 0-672-31796-6. There may also be other books on the subject that you could find.

Whether you study Visual InterDev or ColdFusion is up to you and what is more in demand in your locale. Personally, I have made a decent living with Microsoft products, and despite what some people say (Even Saints have had enemies and people that spread bad rumors about them) I like Visual InterDev. I cannot, however, say that it is a perfect product. Sometimes strange things happen when you are using software and Visual InterDev is no exception.

Along with the Server-side scripting you need to find out how ColdFusion or Active Server Pages place data in and take data out of a database. Putting data into and taking it out of a database is often all that business software does, and it is a good thing to learn and know cold.

At this point you can probably get an entry-level position somewhere. You should be able to create a Web Site, put JavaScript in it, take data from a web page and put it into a database on the server, take that data out again and display it on another web page, and possibly create some reports for management.

While you may be able to get an entry-level position somewhere this is by no means where you should stop your self-study. You should probably learn XML, PERL, and even how to manipulate pictures and images. You will, at least, need to be able to change the sizes of images and various other basic tasks. You can't call up an artist or Graphic Designer every time you need a picture shrunk a little bit.

An additional resource you might find useful is a magazine entitled "Web Techniques". Their web address is www.webtechniques.com or you can call them at (415) 947-6000. Another magazine that you might be interested in is "Internet". Look for it in a bookstore along with other computer magazines. There are so many magazines and web sites that are of use to you, just do some searching on the search engines like Yahoo and you'll find them.

CHAPTER 5

NETWORK ADMINISTRATION

The first rule in supporting a network is to always look for the cause of something yourself, and to not assume the user knows what is wrong.

You should listen to a user to find out *what happened*, but *not* to get their opinion as to what the cause is. I'm not saying you should be rude. Listen to everything the User has to say out of politeness, but you're the expert in networks and so it is your job to figure out what is wrong and fix it.

Ahhh...Networking. This was my first love (other than my wife). When I decided to get into computers, I did not have any well-defined plan on exactly what I wanted to do or where I wanted to end up. That is partly why I am writing this book. To assist someone else who may be in the same shoes I was in and have no clear idea of what to do.

While I was going to school I got tired of making only a little above minimum wage. So, while taking my college classes I studied books and magazines written for beginners in computers. However, so many people think of computers as mysterious boxes that any knowledge about PCs puts you above a lot of people. Well, lucky for you. Someday computers won't be a mystery to anyone, and computer professionals will need to know a lot more than they do now.

Okay, so your objective in this chapter is to learn what you need to study and how to study it so that someone will pay you real money to take care of all their business's PCs and other microcomputers.

This would be a good time to define some words:

- **Microcomputer**: the smallest and least powerful of the three main types of computers. An example is a PC or a Macintosh.
- **Mainframe**: the other two types of computers are a **Mainframe** and a **Mini-computer**. Mainframes are the largest of all computers and are what you see in the movies that line the wall of a sterile-looking room and have spinning rolls of tape. An IBM 370, or 390 would be one example.
- A **Minicomputer** would be in between these other two. Not quite a mainframe but more powerful than a microcomputer. The distinction between these three types of computers is becoming blurred as the power of PCs (microcomputers) is increasing. The power of some desktop PCs has even far surpassed the power of mainframes in the 1970's. And depending on the PC, you might be able to add enough hardware to match mini-computers and maybe some mainframes.
- **Workstation**: This is just a PC that is usually at a business and is intended for work, as opposed to playing games, etc. Often workstations are somewhat more powerful than home PCs as the workstations may need to do more math ("Number Crunching"), or move more graphics (pictures) around, which requires the computer to do more work.
- **PC**: Just in case you don't know a "PC" is just a **Personal Computer**. In other words a Microcomputer. A Macintosh is actually a personal computer also but often when someone says "PC" they mean a personal computer that has a processor made by Intel. These days PCs are very powerful compared to computers in the past. But just twenty years ago (has it been that long?) PCs were just playthings for electronics hobbyists. Some useful things to do on those old home computers had been discovered but not too many.
- **Hardware**: Hardware is all the electronic parts of a computer that you can touch.

- **Software**: Programs that run on the computer are called software. Floppy disks are not considered hardware or software, but instead are called "media".

A Simple Idea

As I have already mentioned earlier, a network is just two or more computers connected together. And this allows them to communicate and exchange information. One example would be the Internet. This is just one big international network and nothing more.

You can see that the network itself is a simple idea. But if in reality they were that simple, no one would pay you to take care of their network. But more of that in a minute. Later I'll refer you to a couple of books that will tell you how to build a computer. It isn't really that hard. But right now I want to explain the hardware and software required to get a network going.

The Hardware of a Network

If you were to take the back off of a PC you would find some slots in a large circuit board (motherboard) that makes up most of your computer. There are probably other circuit boards (also called "cards") that are stuck into some of these slots.

As you can see from looking at the back of your computer, there is a plug-like hole on a Network card (NIC) that looks a lot like a telephone jack. In fact, if you pull the telephone cord out of the wall at your home (remember to push down on the little locking piece sticking out) you would see the same type of piece that you would stick into the back of a networking card. However, the telephone jack won't work in a network card. Even though the telephone cable itself will, the jack won't.

Take a look at your telephone jack. Go ahead and do that right now. Do you see how the jack has four little slots in it? That jack is used for telephones and is called an "RJ-11" connector. A Network card uses an "RJ-45" connector. This type of connector (or jack) has eight little slots in it. If you look at the plug-like hole on the back of a network card you'll see eight wires. This is how you tell the difference between an RJ-11 and an RJ-45 connector.

There are a number of different types of networks. One is called **Token Ring** and another is called **Ethernet**. This only refers to the *physical* way the cables are set up and the way the pieces of information are *physically* passed around the network.

At this time you only need to know about Ethernet, as most of the businesses that you may start working at will probably be using that type of network. In may be true that all businesses, excluding the huge older companies and the government, all use Ethernet. I couldn't say for a fact, but it appears to me that this is true. I don't think many companies still use Token Ring.

Again let me stress the importance of getting dictionaries on everything related to computers. Don't try to save $10.00 or $15.00 by not buying a book you need when that $15.00 will make you many thousands of dollars over your lifetime.

One dictionary I can recommend is "Novell's Dictionary of Networking" by Peter Dyson. Sybex and Novell Press publish this book. The ISBN Number is 0-7821-1494-6. Another book that may help is "Encyclopedia of Networking". Publisher: Sybex. ISBN #: 0-7821-1829-1.

OK, so now you have a network card (Network Interface Card or "NIC" for short) inside the computer, and the connector (RJ-45) for the cable. But, of course, you also need cable to connect the computers together.

Cable is not cable is not cable. One size cable doesn't fit all. There are actually nine grades of cable. Category 1 and 2 you don't need to worry about. It is used for telephones and won't be used for a network. Category 3 and Category 5 (called "cat 3" or "cat 5") are the types of cable generally used in Ethernet networks. Category 3 cables are used for 10-Megabit networks. A Megabit is a little over one million bits and there are eight bits in a Byte. So this type of cable will carry about 125,000 bytes per second between computers.

A bit is just a "0" or "1" in computer talk. Actually a "1" would just mean there was some electricity in the wire traveling through it. If you dropped a stone in a lake, each of the ripples would be a "1" and the depression between each wave would be a "0" or a lack of electricity.

So Cat 3 cable would carry 10 million of these "0"s or "1"s per second. A Cat 5 cable would be appropriate for a 100-Megabit network. 100-Megabit networks are more expensive to set up and are usually more than most businesses need, so you'll probably work on a 10 Mbps (Megabits per second) network. But having Cat 5 cable installed is a good idea even if you only have a 10 Mbps network, as you may want to upgrade later.

So far we have almost all the hardware we need for a network. We have a Network card (NIC, pronounced "Nick", also called a Network Adapter by some), the RJ-45 connectors, and some cable to connect it all together. But one thing is missing for a basic network. This piece of hardware is called a "hub". You can buy these in computer stores or in catalogs devoted to computer and network equipment. A hub will have sockets to connect the RJ-45 connectors into. These RJ-45 connectors are on the other side of the cable that you have plugged into your computer. And a hub can have four or more sockets. As long as you have two computers plugged into a hub you have a network.

The Software of a Network

So far we have the physical requirements for a network. But the most important part of a network is the software that makes communication between computers possible.

Just because I say that the software side of it is more important, don't let that fool you. If the physical requirements are not established, then it won't matter what the software will try to do. It still won't work.

One of the most obvious and possibly least thought of solutions to the problem of a user not being to connect to your network is that the network cables are not plugged into the back of the user's PC or the jack on the wall. Remember that a workstation or the cables are often under the user's desk. So they might kick them in the normal course of work, and the connections often come loose, whether or not the cable actually comes out of the computer. They may not look loose but you may want to unplug and then plug them in again. Trust me, it happens far more than you might think.

Now you have the physical part of the network ready, but in order to run a network you need to install the programs that actually do the real work of communicating between computers.

The software (programs) that you will install on the Workstation is called the "client" software. It's only called "Client" software because each computer acts like a client to other computers on the network when it requests data from them.

Before I can talk about installing the client software I really need to talk about the major types of networks businesses have installed.

There are really three major types of networks. These are **Microsoft Windows Networks**, **Novell Networks**, and **UNIX** operating system networks. You can also have a **Macintosh network** but I have only run into one of these in my career.

The UNIX network is something most small to medium businesses won't use unless they are companies that deal with the Internet. If you want to learn about this type of network then there are plenty of books in the computer section of your local bookstore that will teach you about it.

Most workstations at a business will have some form of Microsoft Windows installed on them. This could be Windows NT 4, Windows 95, Windows 98, or the newest version of Windows 2000 Professional or Server.

This doesn't mean that you have a Windows network. It just means that the operating system software on the workstation is Microsoft Windows. Even though Windows is on the workstations, you can still have a Novell network, a Macintosh network, a Windows network, or even a UNIX network. Remember the network software is not the same as the software that is on the workstations (PCs).

There are actually two ways you can setup a network. You can just have a bunch of workstations connected together; No workstation on this network would have any special status over any other workstation. They would all just be able to talk to each other, share files, share a printer, etc. This would be called a **Peer-to-Peer** network. Each computer is a *peer* of each other. In other words they are all equal.

The other type of network setup is where you actually have a computer, usually a more powerful computer, be in charge of such things as security (for example letting people onto the network, holding User's files to make backing up the data easier, etc.

This computer would be called the "Server" or "File Server". A File Server and a Server aren't necessarily the same, but computer people use them interchangeably. A File Server is a computer that stores files that are used by many people or programs. Thus it "serves" the files up to the user. A File Server may also take care of network security and the other things that a network operating system does, but it may not. It depends on how you set it up. So the term "Server" is often used to mean a computer that "serves" files up to users, or to mean the computer that is in charge of the network dealing with security, etc., or both. Traditionally a Server is more powerful than a normal workstation as it is doing a lot more work than a computer at somebody's desk.

Installing Client Software

Whether you have a Windows NT, Windows 2000, Novell or Macintosh network you will need to install software on the workstations in order to allow them to connect to the File Server or any other computer.

I will just briefly describe how to set this up on a Windows 95 computer and you'll be able to figure out the differences for the other types of networks. Remember that you should read the installation directions that came with your type of network. The instructions should explain exactly what you need to do. The Computer business is no place for someone who can't or won't follow directions (Though messing with things is one of the fun and best ways to learn something).

Here's how you'd do it:

- Click 'Start' on the bottom left of the screen.
- Click 'Settings'
- Click 'Control Panel'.
- Then double click on the 'Network' icon. Don't worry if a message pops up saying something about your network not being complete. Just click yes to continue.
- Click 'Add' and then double click 'Client'. You may see other things in the 'Configuration' list. If you have already installed a Network adapter then this should be there. If you already have Internet access then your Internet Service Provider may have put things in there also.
- If you are on a Windows NT or just a Windows 98 (or 95) network you would click 'Microsoft' on the left and all the choices would appear on the right. If you're on a Novell network you could either choose 'Microsoft', and use the Microsoft 'Client for NetWare Networks', or you could click on 'Novell' on the left and use one of those choices, or if Novell gave you a floppy disk you could click on 'Have Disk' and use what's on the disk. You don't need to worry about the other choices on the left unless you have a UNIX network, or some other network that is instructing you to use those.
- Because in this example scenario we're on a Windows NT or a Windows 98 network I'm going to choose 'Microsoft' on the left and on the right I'll choose 'Client for Microsoft Networks'.
- After you've selected something on the right click 'OK'.

- You'll probably now be back at the main Network screen. If you are on a Windows 95 or Windows 98 network you don't need to do this step. Skip to the next one. If you're on a Windows NT network you'll need to click 'Client for Microsoft Networks' to highlight it, and then click on 'Properties'. You would need to then check the box that says, 'Log on to Windows NT Domain', and then enter the name of the Domain in the 'Windows NT Domain:' box. The 'Domain' is just the name of the Network that the network was given when it was set up. If you have a Domain set up then you will know what this name is. If you are doing this on someone else's domain you should ask what the Domain name is. Click 'OK' again.

- You still must uniquely identify this workstation on the network. While you may be allowed to name two computers the same name, watch out. It will cause you a lot of trouble very soon. Click on the 'Identification' tab at the top of the main network screen. Put the name the computer will have on the network in the 'Computer Name' box and put the name of its workgroup in the 'Workgroup' box. You can name the workgroup whatever you want, but at this time make sure all the computers on your test network have the same Workgroup name. A Workgroup is just a subdivision of the network that you don't really need to worry about at this point. Then just click 'OK'. You may need to insert floppy disks into the computer (If it asks for them). If the computer asks if you want to keep a file that is already on the computer you would usually answer yes as the one on your computer may be newer than the one you are now trying to install.

- Let me give an example of what you could do with a Workgroup. If you left every computer's Workgroup box blank, then whenever you double-clicked on 'Network Neighborhood' on your Windows 95, Windows 98, Windows NT or Windows 2000 main screen (The Desktop) you would see all of the computers that were on the network.

If, for example you had ten computers on your network and five were in accounting and the other five were sales, you could put 'Accounting' in the workgroup name for the accounting people and 'Sales' in the workgroup name for the Sales people. When you then double-clicked on Network Neighborhood you should see 'Accounting' and 'Sales'. When you then double-clicked on one of those you would see the five people that had been assigned to those workgroups. It just makes administration of the network easier.

• As a side note sometimes you may need to do one extra step in order to be able to see a computer in 'Network Neighborhood'. In the Control Panel go back to the Network icon and double-click again. On that main screen there is one button that says, 'File and Print Sharing'. If your operating system doesn't have this then don't worry about it. If you do have it then click on it and put a check in the box that says, 'I want to be able to give others access to my files'.

What you're doing in the Control Panel is installing the software that actually allows the operating system (Windows 98, Windows 2000, or Windows NT for instance) to talk to the physical hardware.

You also need to do two other things to your computer to get it on a network. You need to go back into the Network icon of the Control Panel and add a network adapter (network card) if one wasn't already installed. The network card (or adapter) needs to be physically in your computer before you install the client software. If a network card isn't already in your computer then just follow the instructions on how to install it that came with it.

Network Protocols

In addition you will need to add a Protocol in the Network icon of the Control Panel. A protocol is nothing more than a language that allows different computers to communicate. And when I say different computers I mean Macintosh, IBM PCs, Mainframes, etc. If each of these types of computers had the same protocol installed on it they would be able to communicate. The three most popular protocols are TCP/IP, NetBEUI, and IPX.

NetBEUI is a Microsoft protocol and is all you need if you just want a Peer-to-Peer network with every workstation running some version of Windows.

IPX is a Novell protocol and isn't really used outside of Novell networks (but can be if you wanted to).

The most popular of all protocols now is TCP/IP. The reason for this is that TCP/IP is the protocol of the Internet. And the world has gone *Internet!* This may just be another fad, as often happens, or it may be permanent. But chances are that even though things change constantly in this business they won't change all that much. You know the saying, "The more things change the more they stay the same."

To install an adapter and protocol you would go to the Network icon of the Control Panel just as you did for the network client. Except in this case you would choose 'Adapter' or 'Protocol' and click on 'OK'. On the left-hand side of the screen you now have a list of the Manufacturers of the Adapter or the company whose version of the protocol you want to use. On the right choose the specific model of adapter (or click on 'Have Disk' and use the manufacturer-supplied disk), or for a protocol click on the specific one you want to use.

If you are a newly hired person working on someone else's network, you should ask what protocol to use. But if you are setting up a network at home in order to learn how to do it then my recommendation is to choose Microsoft on the left-hand side and then choose NetBEUI. This is the simplest choice at this time and you can learn more at a later time. While TCP/IP is most likely the protocol that will be used when you actually get a job, there is a lot more work to get TCP/IP up and running. For one thing you have to assign each workstation a unique address in the format xxx.ccc.ddd.kkk. One example would be 127.0.0.1 (this is the same as

127.000.000.001)(You can't actually assign a computer this address as that address is used for testing the computer that TCP/IP is installed on).

This address has to be unique on the network. So what happens on a network of 10,000 when you accidentally assign two workstations the same IP address? That's when the fun starts! You need to learn more about TCP/IP before you set it up. Windows NT has something called DHCP in the Control Panel that lets you just give it a range of addresses and the Server will assign these addresses to the client computers for you. Don't let it assign an address to a Server. You'll need to assign the Server an address manually. DHCP assigns TCP/IP addresses as they are needed. Which means that the same computer could end up with one address one week and another address another week. With a Server it is crucial that this not happen. When you manually assign the Server, or any computer for that matter, a TCP/IP address, you have assigned it permanently (at least until you manually change it again).

A book that might be useful is "Mastering Home Networking" by Mark Henricks (ISBN: 0782126308). I have not read this book but it looks like it covers what you would need to know. There really isn't much difference between a home network and one at a company. All the principles are the same, just some of the parts are bigger, and more types of hardware may be used. But this is really a minor difference.

Back Up Your Data!!!

The last thing I should mention is actually the most important thing a Network Administrator can do:

The most important thing a Network Administrator can do is to back up all the important data on their network, and verify that it is actually getting backed up correctly.

Doing a back up means using a program that is specifically designed to copy and shrink the data and put it on something for storage, usually a tape cassette or some other form of magnetic tape. This tape is then put somewhere safe, usually in another building, protected from fire.

Not having a back up that is accurate and verified is the only real time that a Network Administrator will get into serious trouble. And by serious trouble I mean getting fired. So, don't ignore this warning.

There are two reasons for a backup. The first, and most important is that if there were a fire or some other catastrophe you would be able to restore the old data to a new server if necessary. The second reason is that someone may find that one of their important files is missing and you can go back and restore that file for them. When you have done this for someone and possibly saved his or her job, you will really feel that you have accomplished something. There is no better feeling than saving another person from a possible catastrophe.

What Should You Do At This Point?

At this point you have decided that you want to work in networking.

You will be looking for an entry-level position at first. Entry-level people generally take care of the hardware problems that occur with workstations, installing modems, etc. They will also take care of the usual problems that network users will call up with such as printers not printing, not being able to connect to the network, a word processing program not working right, etc.

So, you'll need to learn about computer hardware and the operating system software that business workstations will be running. Usually this operating system software will be a version of Windows such as Windows NT or Windows 98. But some businesses may be running UNIX or Macintosh computers, too. Since the majority of businesses will be running Windows, this is the one you should learn well. If they also happen to be running another operating system on their workstations they will probably allow you to learn that on the job.

I can't stress how important it is to have your own computer and not use one at a school or something like that. In fact you really need at least two computers at home to do the networking side of things. Think of it as an investment in your future. That is really what it is. Don't let a few dollars that you don't want to spend now prevent you from making a lot more in the future. Remember what I said before, that at one time in my past I had nothing but two cents in my pocket and some clothes. These days I have a house and two cars (Of course one is for my wife, but don't tell her that!).

There are many Novell networks out there, and many Windows NT networks (Or the new Windows 2000 Server). It seems that the Novell networks are usually the big ones (5,000 or more workstations), and the smaller to midsize are Windows NT. It turns out that UNIX and Linux are very popular as well. I'm sure there are many exceptions to these statements. I'm only giving the impression I have from my experience and what I've read in networking magazines.

My personal belief is that Windows NT networks are superior to Novell NetWare, at least on the administration side of things. But there are many jobs out there that still use Novell, though what I have read is that there are more Windows NT networks than Novell.

Some Additional Books

Some books that might help you get started are:

Title: Networking: A Beginner's Guide
Author: Bruce Hallberg
Publisher: McGraw-Hill Professional
ISBN: 0072122269

Title: Home Networking Visual Jumpstart
Author: Erik B. Sherman

Publisher: Sybex
ISBN: 0782127959

Title: Build Your Own Home Network
Author: Ron Gilster and Diane McMichael Gilster
Publisher: McGraw-Hill Professional Book Group
ISBN: 0072124660

Title: Mastering Home Networking
Author: Mark Henricks
Publisher: Sybex
ISBN: 0782126308

Title: The Essential Guide to Home Networking Technologies
Author: Gerard O'Driscoll
Publisher: Prentice Hall PTR
ISBN: 0130198463

Title: Home Networking Bible
Author: Sue Plumley
Publisher: Hungry Minds, Inc.
ISBN: 0764533991

CHAPTER 6

SOFTWARE DEVELOPMENT

This is a subject that I think many newcomers are confused about. Most people have heard of programming, but most don't know what it really is. Programming is simply when a person, a "programmer", writes instructions for a computer to follow. If you were playing a card game that came with your computer, every time that you clicked on a card the computer would react in some way. A "computer program" is what the computer follows when it is reacting to what you just did while you were playing that card game. A "Programmer" is the person who writes those instructions, and the computer program is also called "Software". Thus "Software Development" is designing and writing a computer program.

The computer instructions that a programmer writes are written in a sort of shorthand notation. An example would be:

```
if (x = 2)
      printf ("Number 1");
else
      printf ("Number 2");
```

This notation also looks something like algebra. But you don't need to know math to do programming unless you write programs that deal specifically with mathematical subjects.

The example above means that if the value that "x" stands for (as in algebra) is equal to two, then "Number 1" will be printed on the screen, otherwise ("else") print "Number 2" on the screen.

There are many different systems of notation for writing programs. These systems are known as "languages". This is probably because you as a programmer are speaking to the computer through the language. The above example was written in a language called "C". There are many languages out there. The more common ones are "C", "C++"(pronounced **See plus plus**), Visual Basic, Visual C++, Smalltalk, and Pascal. Other less common languages include Dylan, Python, Eiffel, Modula 2, and Prolog. PERL is a language that is used to write programs for use on web sites, but it can be used for other things as well.

As in the other parts of this book, the purpose of this section is to get you going in the right direction, not to teach you too much about software development itself. To get yourself in shape to write programs and do software development you will need to study a lot of books. I will explain some basic parts and terminology so that you can make the right choices for your career direction.

To get started you will need to get a modern computer (or build one yourself). You can either get a Macintosh, UNIX, or Microsoft Windows computer. What type of computer you get will probably depend on what the first computer language you decide to learn will be. Many languages run on most major operating systems, but some do not. The main languages that don't are the "Visual" languages. These languages run on Microsoft Windows computers only. There are other languages that also run on Windows 95, 98 and 2000, but the Visual languages like Visual Basic and Visual C++ will only run on Microsoft Windows operating systems.

Don't let this fool you. The Windows operating system is the most popular operating system for home use and Personal Computers. So this may be the area you want to get into. But the world is full of more than Personal Computers. There are also very large computers called **Mainframes**, and a size of computer between a Mainframe and a PC called a Minicomputer. Mainframes and Minicomputers don't generally run the Windows or Macintosh operating system. They run operating systems that belong to just them. And there is a programming language that is generally just used for them called COBOL. You may have heard of it, as it was the cause of the Y2K problem. COBOL was created 40 or so years ago and its creator probably didn't conceive that it would ever last until the year 2000. So he or she shortened the year of the date to just two numbers and that led to all the problems.

COBOL would probably not be a good choice for you to learn, as there are many older programmers out there who have been doing it for many years, and because the Y2K problems are now gone there don't seem to be many jobs left using COBOL. COBOL was the first business language created and there are many other languages out there that are more modern and more useful for today's problems.

A programmer I once knew said, "You have to learn Windows or Macintosh programming to make it". This is probably true though these days you can do a lot of Internet programming using HTML, JAVA, JavaScript and other things like that. You could possibly be more successful than a Windows or Macintosh (Mac) programmer.

If you have decided that you want to write programs then you need to decide whether you want to write programs for Personal Computers such as the one you have at home, the Internet, or the large Mainframes. Actually, many of the same languages could be used on all of these "Platforms" as they are called, but generally companies don't seem to be set up for this. I think this is because managers of IT (Information Technology) Departments sometimes don't have experience in a wide range of computer areas and so they don't know what the current possibilities are for software development. The fundamentals of computers are the same no matter what area you are working in, and some people don't realize that switching from one area of expertise to another is really easier than they think.

What Area Do You Want To Work In?

The first thing that you should look at is what area do you really want to work in? This is always that first and most important thing to be considered. Also, what is your reason for wanting to work in computers and write and design programs?

Maybe you're just plain tired of being poor. Well then, I would recommend starting with the area that appears to have the most jobs. Go out to job web sites such as www.monster.com, or www.dice.com and search for jobs in the different areas I've mentioned. It appears that there are a lot of Internet jobs, and on the PC side there are many jobs that use Visual Basic. But you do your own search as things are constantly changing in the computer world. Some geographic areas also seem to have different requirements. One Head Hunter told me that in Denver all the jobs were for programmers who knew **C**, but that in Southern California everybody wants Visual Basic programmers.

If you have a particular area that you are interested in, or even infatuated with, then by all means concentrate on that area. Having enthusiasm for your job is something that may help you get your first job. And it will help you later when you're working. You should like what you're working in.

What ever the area you choose, remember that all success takes a lot of work. Very seldom does success just accidentally fall into someone's lap. Playing the Lotto may be fun, but you really can't expect to win. Don't treat your career like the Lotto. YOU have to make the changes happen. YOU have to study all those hours, and spend all that time trying to figure out why things don't work. Why do you think computer people have a reputation for making more money than many people make? I think it's because many people aren't willing to put in the effort it takes to learn what they need to learn to be competent at a computer job. Those people that are willing to put the time and effort into becoming competent are rewarded with decent salaries. You don't need to be a genius to be a Software Developer or a Network Administrator, but you do need to learn what is required to do your job and you need to be able to take what you've learned and use it in new situations. In other words, you actually need to be able to *think*. Thinking takes effort. Even on the job you can't just go through the motions like you could if you were a lumberjack. Laziness isn't going to get you anywhere. Sometimes it'll be tough. Just do your best. That's more than many people will do.

If you don't work for a company that has a Mainframe, or if you don't have access to a University with a Mainframe then this option probably isn't for you. The Internet has many opportunities, but you may have heard recently of a lot of Internet companies going broke. There was a time there that if you started a business that had ".com" in it that you could make a fortune, even if the company didn't make a profit. Well, those days seem to be over.

To get an Internet job you generally don't need any college at all. If you know HTML, JAVA, JavaScript, how to administer a web site, and maybe a proprietary language (and by proprietary I mean a single company makes and owns the copyrights on that language. Meaning also that if that company goes out of business the programming language will probably go out of use), such as ColdFusion, or how to write Active Server Pages (ASP), you could probably get an entry-level position somewhere. One of the great things about training for this type of job is that you can create your own web pages, put them on the web, and show prospective employers what you can do. You can get experience easily without anyone paying you, and without spending a lot of money yourself. In fact, if you were to study all of the subjects I just mentioned you would probably have all you needed to get started in this area of software development.

I talked about working on the Internet in an earlier chapter, and if this is what you're interested in you should read that chapter as well.

Now we get to the area of programming that I've always loved. This is called Application Programming. This area would include business programs, games, just about anything that will run on the computer that a User would use directly. There is one other type of programming and that would be called Systems Programming. That would involve writing operating system software. In other words the software that controls the computer's hardware and manages what other programs run on your computer.

This is an interesting area of computers but if you are interested in this you should probably go to college and specialize in that area. There aren't too many jobs that do this sort of programming and employers generally seem to look for college degrees. Of course Bill Gates didn't get a college degree and he's written a great deal of operating system software. But you'll also notice that he started his own company and didn't ask someone else to employ him. You are still very free to learn this area of programming and go write an operating system without any college. But it's a different story when you ask someone else to give you a job.

New Words

Before I go any further I should probably define a couple of terms and explain some of the things that you'll need to teach yourself programming. I've already explained what a programming *language* is, and that is the first thing that you'll need to buy or download off the Internet.

In order to actually get a program ready for the computer to do (also called run or execute), you need to use another software program to change the English-like *Source Code* (the English-like words that you wrote in a programming language) into *executable* (the verb form means: able to be run by the computer. It doesn't understand English after all. The noun means the actual program that is able to be executed by the computer, thus the name executable) *machine language* (the actual code that the computer understands. It is really just a bunch of numbers that stand for *instructions* that the program you wrote is telling the computer to do).

The software program that you would use to change your Source code into executable code is called a *Compiler*. There is also software called an *Interpreter* that does the same thing but in a different way and you don't really need to worry about that. The only thing you need to be aware of is that **compiled** code is faster than **interpreted** code. For *almost* anything you do as a professional you won't use an Interpreter, except for perhaps the mini-language PERL.

At this point the only software you really need to get is a compiler. The source code can be written in any text-editing program that allows you to type in text. If you have a Windows computer you should have two text editing programs already on your computer: One is Notepad and the other is WordPad. The one requirement to this is that you must be able to save it as "text-only". Microsoft Word, Star Office and similar programs usually save their documents with hidden characters that mean special things to their programs but make no sense to any other program. All these programs will usually let you save your text as text-only but if you have unexplained problems later just remember to try another text editor.

An Example

Let's say you've decided to go the mainstream route where there are a lot of jobs. Remember no matter what you decide to do there will be a lot more employers looking for experienced people than entry-level job seekers. So don't let that discourage you in any way. After all, you have nothing to loose if they don't hire you and everything to gain if they do. And you only need *one* employer to offer you a job. The numbers are on your side.

By *mainstream* I mean to say business programs on and for the Microsoft Windows family of operating systems. You've decided to learn Visual Basic. Visual Basic now has a reputation for being able to quickly and easily assemble business applications. For us programmers, that is good public relations and is true to an extent. But as in all things it starts to get more complicated the more you learn. Simple programs are easier to write, and beginners may think the easiest way to do things is the best. But hard experience has taught me that while VB (Visual Basic) may have something built into the language, you may be better off doing it from scratch. Accessing a database for instance. The built in features of VB are there to use but if you want to do anything more than basic access to a database you need to do it yourself. And sometimes those built in features have bugs (parts that don't work right. This term came from a moth being electrocuted inside of an early computer in 1958) that don't do what they are supposed to do.

The first thing to do, other than buy a PC is to get a book on Visual Basic. Go to the bookstore and find the computer section. The larger bookstores have huge sections on everything to do with computers. I've even seen a large section on just getting certified. One book that is good for getting started is **SAMs "Teach Yourself Visual Basic in 21 Days"**. This is a good book for learning your way around Visual Basic and finding out how to do various things. It is a very practical book and falls short as far as theory goes. But you want to first get your feet wet. The last I saw this book didn't have a version of VB that you could put onto your PC. If you don't have VB on your PC you may want to either buy the Standard or Professional versions from Microsoft (www.microsoft.com) or you may want to buy a book set that has the "Learning" edition of VB with it. The Learning edition will be very limited in what you can do and it may not let you compile a program that can be run outside of the Learning Edition Editor. But it will still allow you to learn the basics of VB.

After you have written a bit of VB code and you can compile a program, you'll want to learn something in addition to that. Something that just about every business program needs to do is get data from a database. A database is just a file on the computer that has related data stored together in such a way that you can easily get it when you need it.

In the same section of the bookstore that you found the **SAMs "Teach Yourself Visual Basic in 21 Days"** book you will be able to find a book on VB and Databases. There are a number of different database products on the market and you may be called upon to get data from any one of them. But the way to do that in VB is really about the same.

Databases

Part of learning how to interact with a database is a relatively simple new language that you must learn to extract data from it. No database understands VB or any other programming language (except perhaps Object Oriented Databases like you can find at www.poet.com. But that is something that you shouldn't worry about at this time). This new "language" is called **Structured Query Language**, better known as **SQL**. Some people pronounce each letter separately, while others (including myself) say it as a single word, pronouncing it like the word "sequel".

SQL was originally designed to allow non-programmers to get data out of a database, so it is simpler than a programming language. But it will still take some getting used to if you already know a programming language, and as in all things, you may sometime come across some pretty hairy SQL code (actually they are called "Statements").

Shareware

At this point in your studies you will know some VB and how to get data out of a database. At this point you may now have enough knowledge to get a job. Most employers want experience. Well, you're in luck. As with almost everything in computers you can get all the experience you need in the privacy of your home. Write some programs that might be useful to someone and put it out on the Internet for free at a shareware or freeware site. Two sites that you may want to look at are www.shareware.com, and www.download.com.

As you may have deduced from the name, *Shareware* is software that you share with other people. Sometimes the programmer asks for a small fee from people who like the programs they have downloaded (from the Internet), but the fee is voluntary.

When you go for an interview you could bring your program along or tell the interviewer where on the web it is. If you plan on installing the program on the interviewer's computer make sure you have tested out installing it on a computer other than the one you developed it on. Many things can happen when you move it to another computer. Visual Basic has something that helps you create a setup program called the "Package and Deployment Wizard". This will help you to get all the files together that need to go onto the new computer. One of the advantages of Windows is that the different programs that run on it often share files they need. But every Windows computer doesn't have the same files. So the "Package and Deployment Wizard" puts all the files your program needs into a setup program, which you can then use to install your program on another computer.

But beware of installing a program you wrote on a prospective employer's computer. Many things can go wrong, and if something later gets messed up on the prospective employer's computer, even if it had nothing to do with your program, you may get blamed for it. Its better to take a laptop to the interview that has the program already setup and thoroughly tested on it. That way it will work for the interview and you can't mess up anybody's computer.

After That

After you have read the first couple of books, you need to read another VB book. This is even if, and especially if, you already have a job. If you are already comfortable with the basic VB stuff you've read then you need to read something more advanced. There are books on advanced VB that you could read, or maybe you want to learn more about database design. You definitely need to learn more about general Windows programming. Because Visual Basic runs in the Microsoft Windows operating system there are many areas that you can get into that are outside of VB. Check into these when you feel you're ready. Many programmers seem to go a lot of their career without knowing this advanced stuff. But you want to be better than average, you should strive to be the best. That way even if a lot of people get laid off you will still have a job. And even if you get laid off it will be easier to get another job.

If you are interested in programming Microsoft products you might try a magazine called **Visual Studio Magazine**. Their web site at this time is www.vbpj.com, but by the time you read this it may be something like www.vsm.com. The reason the web site is www.vbpj.com is because the magazine was called **Visual Basic Programmer's Journal** and it's changing its name. It will now feature articles on all of the Visual Studio products.

Is There Something Other Than Visual Basic I Can Work In?

Of course there is. I was just using that as an example and because I have experience in that area. There are many areas that you can program in. One thing that you may have heard of is the JAVA programming language. This is a hot area these days. I have heard stories of two different people that I used to work with who learned JAVA and with no experience went off to make huge salaries. At least one of those stories is probably true. The other I have no way of verifying.

The strategy for what to learn for JAVA is basically the same as Visual Basic. But of course you would get a book such as SAMs "Teach Yourself JAVA in 21 Days"(ISBN: 0672319586). And next you would get a book on JAVA and databases. While there are JAVA jobs that are not related to the Internet, JAVA has been associated with the Internet from the beginning. The reason for this is that you can write a small JAVA application that runs inside of a Browser called an "Applet". So it would be a good idea to learn something about HTML and other Internet related material (see the section in this book on the Internet and Web Development).

JAVA will work on Microsoft Windows, Linux (a free version of a UNIX like operating system. To get it try www.linux.com), and the Solaris SPARC workstation made by SUN. In a browser it will work anywhere the browser works.

LINUX is pretty hot these days and you may want to see if there is demand for programmers in your area who know JAVA for the Linux operating system (also known as the Linux Platform, just as Microsoft Windows is known as the Windows Platform).

What ever your choices for a JAVA book remember that there are many, many out there. On one online bookstore I searched for "JAVA" and I came up with over 1300 books. As a beginner it may be a good idea for you to go to a bookstore and look at the books before you buy them. But the "21 Day" books are decent for getting started.

You Are The Expert

Let my final comment to you on the subject of Software Development be this; you are the expert in this field. And unless your boss has done the same study and training that you have even he or she will not be as much of an expert in programming and software development as you are. Your job will be to come in and develop a program or set of programs, and possibly a complete computer "system" that will do for your customer what they want. Your attitude should be and needs to be that anything can be done that the customer wants. This isn't just an attitude it's the truth. When you have the confidence that you will be able to provide to your customer what ever they want no matter what it is, then you will be an expert. Experts are people that can do the job when no one else can. That should be your goal.

Now, I don't say this because I want to be a salesman to the customer. I say this because I know it is the truth. I'm also not saying that I have every book on computers memorized and can do anything without looking at a book. What I am saying is that with current technology you can create any system they need, it just depends on how much work it will take to get the program done. Maybe a customer doesn't want to pay for that extra 100 hours it takes to put psychedelic colors in the program, but you are still able to do it if they are willing to spend the money. Also the speed of the program may not be what they wanted but you can still DO what they want.

The point is that if you don't know how to do it, then go do some research. Look through every book you can find, ask on the Internet newsgroups (this can really help especially if you are the only person working on the program or if no one else at your work knows how to do something either), ask everyone at your work, call up old High School or college teachers, old bosses, that nerd down the street who never comes out of his house because he's always on the Internet, etc. The answer is out there; you just have to find it (hey, was that a flying saucer?)

Chapter 7

Certification

At this point let me introduce the concept of Certification. Certification means that you have taken a test that certifies that you know the subject that you were tested on.

Networking

While there are many certification programs around, certification seems to be most useful in the area of networking.

Certification is beneficial to all people on all sides of the employment question. For an employer, the Human Resources people will be able to see that a prospective employee has the knowledge that they need to do the job. With Certification the Human Resources personnel don't need to have any technical knowledge themselves (Most don't and seem to be there just to evaluate if you would make a good employee. They generally don't have a clue whether you can do your job, so certification is good for this reason).

These days there are many certification programs available. For networking, the main programs are:

- Microsoft Certified Systems Engineer (MCSE) and Microsoft Certified Professional (MCP)
- Certified Novell Engineer (CNE) and Certified Novell Administrator (CNA)
- Microsoft Certified Database Administrator (MCDBA)
- A+ Certification

If you already know where your interests lie, your job of deciding which area to work on is much easier. For instance, if you are already work in a networking department that uses Novell, you may want to work on the CNE (Certified Novell Engineer) series of tests. But its important to work on what you want to work on, not necessarily what you think you'll make more money at.

The MCSE is a series of six tests that culminate in being certified as a Microsoft Certified Systems Engineer. When you pass **one** of these tests you will be granted Microsoft Certified Professional (MCP) status and will be able to use the logo that goes with it on your business cards, stationary, resumes, etc.

You can get information on the MCSE tests on the web at *http://www.microsoft.com/trainingandservices/default.asp* or in the United States at the phone number (800) 636-7544. They also have an e-mail address for certification, which is: mcp@msprograms.com.

If the above web address doesn't work by the time you read this then just go to the main Microsoft web site of www.microsoft.com and click on *Training and Certification.*

The MCDBA tests are for Database Administrators and from what I hear this is a good career option as well as the three I've already mentioned: Web Development, Network Administration, and Software Development. If you want to specialize in Database Administration look for MCDBA information in the same places that you would find the MCSE data.

You can also check out the MCP Magazine web site at www.mcpmag.com for Microsoft certification information.

There is more than one path you can take in certification at Microsoft and Novell. There are different Server products that are out there and you can get certified in which ever suits you particular needs. For example, the latest Server operating system that Microsoft has at this time is Windows 2000 Server. If you don't have any certifications and you don't work in a networking or Information Technology department at this time then you should get certified in the latest and newest Server operating system that Microsoft has. In this case it's Windows 2000 Server. If, however, you now work in a computer department and they use Windows NT 4 then you might consider getting certified in that. The one thing to keep in mind when deciding which to do is that after a while an exam will be "retired". This means you can no longer use if for your MCSE certification and you will have to take another test to replace it. This is how your knowledge is kept up to date and someone hiring you will know that you know the modern programs and not something from years ago.

If you want to go for Novell certification then go to www.novell.com. Novell has a number of networking products also. Which you study will depend on whether you are currently working in a department that uses an older version of Novell or not. But while Microsoft products are simply replaced by newer ones and a company that had an older version of Windows NT will replace it with a newer version, Novell's situation is unique. When Novell came out with NetWare 3.11 and NetWare 3.12 they got a lot of business. In fact, in the beginning, they were the only real network operating system out there specifically for businesses and they really didn't have much competition. My first certification was in NetWare 3.12.

But then Novell came out with NetWare 4.0 and things got a lot more complicated for the Network Administrator. It is probably for this reason as well as the fact that NetWare 3.12 was a very stable operating system that most Novell customers didn't replace 3.12 with 4.0. Not too long ago 66% of the NetWare networks were still NetWare 3.12 and only 34% or so were NetWare 4.0. Novell has recently come out with NetWare 5.0. I think it's too soon to tell whether Novell will gain any of its former customers back with this or not. They have lost a good amount of business to Windows NT and Windows 2000 Server, as well as Linux (a free version of UNIX).

Let's say you want to get certified in NetWare 5.0. The first thing you should do is to take the Certified Novell Administrator (CNA) test for

NetWare 5. Look at this web address for information on becoming a CNA for Novell 5: www.novell.com/education/ certinfo/cna/nw5.html. This is one test and you can then call yourself a CNA. At this point you may even be able to get a job just with that title.

But after that you may want to go all the way and become a CNE (Certified Novell Engineer or Certified NetWare Engineer. What CNE stands for has changed sometimes). This is a series of tests that you have to take and at the end you will be an official CNE. Take a look at www.novell.com/education for all the information you need on Novell certification.

Let me stress that you don't want to become a "Paper CNE" or "Paper CNA". That means that you can answer all the questions on the tests but that you don't really know how to take care of the network. Don't take this to mean that learning the theory that allows you to pass the exams is bad. It just means that there is more to network administration than being able to answer technical questions.

A Company by the name of PROMETRIC, gives the tests that you are most likely interested in taking. The phone number that you can use to sign up for these tests is 1-800-RED-EXAM.

Also another company by the name of Transcender (www.transcender.com) offers a lot of practice exams that are really good for preparing for these tests. The practice exams from Transcender are rather expensive but they are worth the money. Think of all the time you have spent or will spend on getting ready for an exam and compare that to the cost of practice exams.

You can get other practice exams that cost less or may even be free. The Microsoft Certified Magazine is a good place to look for advertisements, or try their web site www.mcpmag.com.

Other Certifications

There are many other certification programs than the MCSE, CNE and A+.

For Software Developers you might consider getting JAVA certification or becoming an **MCSD** (Microsoft Certified Solution Developer).

One of the side benefits of certification is that it looks good on a resume, and more importantly you learn a lot of stuff while you're studying that you may not have ever learned otherwise.

There are a number of books on JAVA certification but one that might be useful is "A Programmer's Guide to JAVA Certification", ISBN: 0201596148. Publisher: Addison-Wesley. And you can check out SUN Microsystems' web site at www.sun.com. They are the main driving force behind getting JAVA accepted in the computer world and you can get the JAVA compiler for free off the web site. That is another good reason for studying JAVA. Most, if not all the materials needed to learn it are free.

You can learn about the MCSD certification in the same place that you can learn about the MCSE certification. Try www.microsoft.com and click on the link for Training and Certification. This certification is good if you are going to work in programming "shops" that use a lot of Microsoft software.

I have not been able to uncover too much information on getting certified for Web Development and the Internet. Microsoft has certification for Web Server Administration but this seems to be more geared towards the Network Administration side of things than actually developing Web Pages.

If Web Development certification is something that you are interested in you may want to surf the net for a while. Maybe you'll find something useful. I did find one certification program that the people at Novell referred me to. A company runs it by the name of Prosoft and you can get information on their certification program at www.computerprep.com and www.cip2ciw.com. Transcender has some practice exams for this certification that you may find useful also.

CHAPTER 8

FINDING YOUR FIRST JOB

So now you have what you think is enough knowledge to get a job. Just by reading and understanding a couple of the books previously mentioned you probably know more than most people.

I got my first job doing Technical Support on the telephone, by just reading a couple of articles in a computer magazine. That combined with what I knew about DOS got me an interview for a better job than the one I had applied for. Out of sixty people who had come into this educational software company for a summertime software testing position only two of us were asked for interviews for Technical Support positions. Those two or three magazine articles gave me the edge.

The secret to job hunting is really a mathematical problem. The more resumes you send out the greater chance you have to get an interview. And the more interviews you have the better your chances to get a job. And don't think ten or twenty resumes are a lot. When I was just getting my College degree I sent out over one hundred resumes and only got four responses. And of those, two were phone interviews and I never heard from them again.

The first thing that you have to do is get a resume. Don't go out and buy books on how to do your resume unless you just want to see the format that some of the recommended resumes are in. Many word processing programs have a resume form (template) that you may find useful. Other than the content of the resume, how it is presented is also important. If you are submitting your resume electronically (through the Internet) there is only so much you can do to make your resume look good. Most resumes that are electronically submitted are just in text (ASCII) format with no fancy fonts or graphics. But when you go for an interview and take your resume (always take a few nicely printed resumes for the interviewers) make sure the resume looks good. By this I mean don't photocopy, or print your resume out on a bad printer. It should look good and be readable. Some of the resumes I have reviewed in the past looked so bad that I had a difficult time believing someone would allow himself or herself to be presented in such a bad light.

When you first start out in a new field you won't have any experience in what you're trying to get a job in (other than what you got at home, which in computers is still good). So, with your resume that presents a problem. Since you do not have any experience it would not be wise to stress that in your resume. So, what you must stress are your abilities, capabilities, education, and *what you can do*, whether you've been paid for it or not. You'll hear many different opinions about how a resume should look, but what's really important on a resume is what it contains.

What is really important in the computer industry now is not how much college you've had, nor even how many jobs you've had, but what you can do. And because you can do so much with computers in your own home by reading books and experimenting, you many have many more things that you can do than what you've learned in school. The end result is the same. You are able to do things whether or not you have a certificate or a diploma. And this is what employers want in today's computer job market. The reason for this is the scarcity of qualified computer people.

So, stress you capabilities. On my resume I usually start with an objective, and then I have a category called **Capabilities**. I use bullets for each of my capabilities and say all of the things that I know and can do. Many of these things I have never done in a paid job. Nonetheless, I still know how to do these things.

Here is an example of how your resume might look stressing your capabilities:

Santa Claus
1 Main st.
North Pole, AK
(555) 555-5555   E-Mail: sclaus@northpole.com.pl

OBJECTIVE

To secure a position as a Software Engineer or Business Programmer

CAPABILITIES

- Wrote Tic-Tac-Toe game in Visual Basic 6
- Wrote stock market tracking program using a combination of Visual Basic and Access 97.
- Program in **Visual Basic 6** using Oracle8, Microsoft SQL Server, and Access97 as back ends.
- Wrote stored procedures in SQL Server 6
- Database design in SQL Server 6.5, Oracle8, and Access97
- Program in C++ and C
- Wrote Active Server Pages (ASP) using Visual InterDev, JavaScript, and VBScript
- Familiar with HTML
- Coursework in Java 1.2
- Coursework in Operating System Design Theory, Database Design, Data Structures, Algorithms, Hardware Organization, Object-Oriented System Analysis and Design
- Some knowledge of the LINUX and UNIX operating systems

CERTIFICATION

- Microsoft Certified Visual Basic 6
- Microsoft Certified Professional (Windows 2000)
- Certified Novell Administrator 3.12

EDUCATION

University of Alaska: Fairbanks, Alaska
Bachelor of Science in Software Engineering, June 2001

WORK EXPERIENCE

August 1998-
Present

Help Desk
Computer Science Lab Univ. of Alaska: Fairbanks, AK
Helped fellow students solve computer related problems at the University computer lab. This involved solving problems related to remote connections over the telephone, networking problems related to the lab itself, printing problems, and helping students with homework problems in programming.

So when you get into a job interview and somebody asks you what you can do, and then asks if you were paid for this, make sure that you stress that you are competent in that area even if you weren't paid for it (be diplomatic). And make sure that you really are able to work on the things that you put on your resume. Honesty. Don't lie. You will not be comfortable if you get a job doing things that you don't know how to do. This is not to say that you can't study really fast at home after you have gotten the job (if you already know something about the subject but you just don't remember the details), I'm just saying that if you cannot quickly brush up on something then you should not lead employers to believe that you know something that you do not.

At this point in time you are lucky to have one asset for your job search that wasn't available just a short time ago. And that asset is the Internet. There are some web sites out there that once you post your resume on many Recruiters (Head Hunters) will automatically receive it. Two job sites that are good are www.monster.com and www.dice.com. There is another site that is only for companies themselves, no Recruiters. That site is www.hotjobs.com. There are fewer listings on that site but the ones that match your qualifications may be better quality. I, at least, have found it so.

You may or may not get many calls. Some of these Recruiters don't really read your resume very well before they call and they may think you know things you don't. Even if you are a fit for one of the jobs they are looking to fill, and they tell you they will submit your resume to a company, you still may never hear from them again. Remember that these are people who will submit your resume to actual employers and if you are hired will receive a commission from the employer (never from you). The problem is that they may submit twenty or thirty resumes for the same job, and the employer may only pick three or four to call in for an interview. Most Recruiters will not call you back to tell you an employer wasn't interested. They just deal in numbers and often lack personal skills.

Don't be discouraged. You only need one job, so you just need to find that one employer out there that wants to hire you. Kind of like marriage, there is someone out there for you no matter how bleak it may look. I found my wife in Czechoslovakia. You probably won't have to go that far.

Your First Job

When you're job-seeking take the first decent job offered to you. Maybe the pay won't be good, maybe the company isn't the best, and maybe you have to drive too far to get to work each day. But remember that when a company hires you, and you have no experience of any kind, that they are taking a chance on you just as you are taking a chance on them.

And when you get some experience, you can begin to consider changing jobs somewhere else. At that time you will have experience and could possibly get better pay as well. But that first job is the hardest to get. And you should not be too picky.

At the company that I was formerly at, we offered a job to an individual that had a degree in a non-computer-related field and a certificate in computer programming. This person had no experience of any kind and yet was asking for exorbitant sums of money. And even worse, he was taking his time on getting back to us after we offered him the job. This person was apparently just waiting for a better offer from somebody else. I had decided a couple of days before we found out that he would not be working with us that even if he had accepted the offer, I would not want to work with him. Obviously he didn't feel like working with us.

After you get your first job, don't think that you're now on easy street. You still don't have time to slack off. With your first job you'll now gain experience, but you still don't have the knowledge to be able to run everything by yourself.

Study, Study

Now that you have a job you will want to study those things needed to do this job well. All learning is really a balance between theory and practice. You need to continue to learn the theory behind the things that you are doing. Experience is only good for becoming comfortable doing the tasks that you know how to do. Experience only teaches you a few new things, whereas theory teaches you many things that you can now go out and "practice". On-the-job training, by itself, is a very limited way to learn things. Do you see what I'm saying?

After you have learned all about the things that you are now doing on your current job, you need to learn everything else that you would need to know to be able to run the whole show on your own. That's when you can decide to take a temporary break in your personal training. This is when you can relax a little bit. But the computer business is always changing, always advancing, and you'll always need to study the new things that come along. That is part of the curse of a fast-moving and new industry. The fact that you can never consider yourself 100 percent trained. But at the same time, this gives you the edge over many other people who don't feel like learning anything new. They just want to keep plodding along in their jobs until they can retire and do nothing but sit on their front porch.

I don't think those people are very happy. You always are doing something even if it's just sitting there doing nothing. That's what life is. This book isn't about how to be happy in life, but considering that you are working the majority of your waking hours, maybe this book really is about life. If you can find a job you like and you feel you are doing something useful, as well as being paid well, why then maybe you would be happy.

This may be your goal, as it may be for all of us, but you can be picky when you have experience and are in great demand. That's when you can pick and choose. Not when you first start out.

Volunteer

If you are worried about your level of experience then go volunteer somewhere. Don't be like this actor I once knew who wouldn't do a single bit of acting unless he was paid. Well, you've never heard of him, and I've never seen him in the movies or TV, and maybe that's why.

There are many places to volunteer. Try a local school, fire department, and your local optometrist who has such ancient computer software that you could whip up something useful in a couple of weeks (free). Maybe you could even sell that software to other optometrists and use the first one as a reference.

Interviews

If you are nervous about interviews, then don't be. The first few interviews may just be practice for you. If, after the interview, you start kicking yourself in the backside because of something you did or didn't say, then just decide not to make the same mistake the next time. That's all you need to do. Eventually you'll get it right and mistake or not you'll find that employer who you will click with and you'll get the job.

Always be as presentable as you can be on interviews. Wear a suit and tie and have a haircut. Even if you wear your hair long it should at least not be scruffy looking. Woman should wear something business-like. Try not to be late to an interview. Sometimes this is hard to do in big city traffic jams or because of the weather, but do your best. No one can ask for more.

Usually the first interview you get with a company is with the Human Resources department. This will not be a technical interview. You may be asked all sorts of questions that have nothing to do with the job you are applying for. As far as I can tell, and from the Human Resources textbooks I have been acquainted with, this interview is to determine how you react and if you would work well in a group. Apparently they don't want someone who is as intelligent as Einstein if they are too much of an individual. I guess the fact that all the major advances in science were always made by an individual doesn't make a difference to Human Resources. And, also the fact that programming and many other computer jobs are really an individual activity, has no bearing on it either. There seems to be some tension between many Human Resource departments and the Information Technology departments. Maybe this is why.

Be prepared for questions like "What do you see yourself doing in five years?" and "What TV or movie character do you see yourself as?". The first question is to determine if you will still be with the company in five years and I guess the second one is to find out what kind of a person you are.

If you get past that interview you will now probably have an interview with someone who you will work with or for. They may ask you technical questions and they may not. They may have someone else ask you the technical questions while they, themselves, may just talk to you and find out if you would do well in their department.

Always be yourself in the interviews with the people you will be working with. If, for some reason, they don't think you will fit in then maybe you shouldn't work there. And this is the time for you to ask questions too. You need to determine if this is a place you would want to work at. You don't want to be uncomfortable in a job that you spend so much of your day in. But remember not to be too picky if this is your first job in the computer field.

Sometimes, you may need to take a test or two. Sometimes the tests are written and sometimes you may get three guys all asking you questions at what seems like machine gun speed. You'll probably make mistakes; don't worry about it. This isn't a war and countless lives don't depend on you doing everything right. It's just an interview.

A Job Offer Comes Your Way

Eventually you'll get an offer from some company. It should be in writing. Sometimes they may offer you a job on the phone and them send the written offer through the mail. It is normal practice to give you a few days to consider if you want to take the job or not. I don't think many people would expect you to make a snap decision and accept the offer right when they offer it. You may be considering other jobs as well (you can only hope).

Your First Day

On your first day of work always wear the most professional clothes you can. Your best bet is a Business suit for men, and a Business suit or professional looking dress for women. It's always better to over dress than to under dress.

If this is your first job in this new career of yours try to be a little conservative at first. Get to know the different people you will be working with, and don't act like you know better than they do (even if you really do). Let them get to know you too. You will have to prove to them that you are competent and know what you're talking about. This can be a really frustrating time period. If you see a better way to do something or if you see a flaw in the way things are being done, technically or not, make a diplomatic suggestion on how it should be done. But if no one will listen, or if the person that is in charge decides to do something different, then let it go. When it's your turn to be in charge then you can make the decisions.

GOOD LUCK!

This little chapter has taken you from the beginning of your job-hunting trek to the first few months of your first job. Your experiences may be completely different from mine, but hopefully this will at least have prepared you for the possible adventures and misadventures that await you on your new career.

CHAPTER 9

SOME ADVICE

In closing, I would like to share some advice that I have found valuable. Some of these things relate to computers and some do not, but I just thought I would mention them. My idea in writing this book was to write down what I would say if someone were interested in changing his or her job to something in the computer industry, or if he or she just wanted a computer career and didn't want to go to college. So, here's what I have to say:

New Terminology

When you are reading books on computers sometimes you may find new words that you are not familiar with. The most important thing you can do in this situation is to find out what that new word means. I must have seven or eight computer dictionaries alone, and I own four regular English dictionaries, as well as slang dictionaries, accounting dictionaries, and any other kind of dictionary that might relate to the work I do. **ALWAYS** find out what a new word means. You really can't understand what you're reading if you don't.

Sometimes when you're talking to people about computers some of these people will start throwing technical words around. Sometimes these are just words that you haven't heard. The important thing is to find out what these words mean so you can understand what is being talked about. Many times you don't even need to read a book on the subject. You just need to look up the words in a good dictionary and from that paragraph in the definition you now understand how it relates to other things in computers.

That brings me to what seems like a problem in some computer books. Sometimes authors will start using words that relate to the subject they are talking about, but they have not yet defined what those words mean. This is usually just an oversight and unintentional. But it sometimes happens that an author will make their own words up and will not define what they mean anywhere in the text. I don't say this to be cynical. I say this from my experience of looking the word up in all of these dictionaries I own, going out onto the Internet, and numerous other ways that I have tried to find out what these words mean, and I eventually just have to figure out what the author meant. I own approximately 100 books on computers not including my dictionaries. And I still could not find out what these words mean. So just be aware of this possibility when you cannot find out what a word means.

College

Another thing I would like to say is that very little of what I do in my job I learned in college. I write Visual Basic programs, I work with databases, I administer databases, I work with mainframes and UNIX machines, and I was designing a system that spanned half the globe. Some colleges today do teach you many things that are useful, but universities always take time to catch up to the real world and you cannot depend on what they teach you as being the most up-to-date.

I'm not saying that college is a bad idea, but what I am saying is that even after you get your degree you will need to study certain areas more in-depth and thoroughly. Having a degree may help you get more job interviews and in the long run higher paying jobs, but it won't teach you more than you can learn on your own just studying books. Remember that I started the hard way. I may now have a degree, but I was already working in networking by the time I received it.

Working a Job Alone

Sometimes you'll find yourself out in the world in a job all by yourself. There won't be anybody else to help you when you don't know what to do. You will rely solely on the knowledge you have gained from studying and the books that you will keep close to you at work.

But sometimes you just don't know what to do. So, where do you go for help? Well, you actually find yourself in a lucky position. The Internet connects you to all kinds of people interested in computers. There are newsgroups and many Web pages that you can find information on.

The way to find information on the Internet is by using Search Engines. Search engines are places like www.yahoo.com, www.infoseek.com, www.northernlight.com and other sites like that. By typing in information that you're looking for, and clicking on the **Search** button, you can find many things that will help you out. Explore these search engine sites. That's the only way to really get to know them. Use the help features that are available at each web site. Each web site has a different way of doing searches and you'll need to read what to do for that particular site.

Possibly the most useful resource that you might find on the Internet are newsgroups. This is an area on the Internet where you can leave a message, which is called "posting a message". Another individual will come along and possibly answer the question that you have put in the newsgroup. The person answering your message may know what could be done to help you out. Just as you could post an answer to somebody else's message if you knew the answer.

If you were using the Netscape Navigator browser then to get to the newsgroups you would click on the menu item "communicator", and then the "messenger" menu item, which would bring you to the newsgroups. You'll probably need to call your Internet Service Provider (such as AOL, CompuServe or Microsoft network) and ask them to help you with setting up your newsgroup program.

Before you can actually see the messages in the newsgroup you'll need to "subscribe" to a newsgroup. All newsgroups are listed in a style such as "comp.network.linux". This basically shows that there is a newsgroup about the operating system Linux, under a sub group called "network", under an overall group called "comp" which stands for computer. For example if you want to find a newsgroup about the computer language "C" you might go to the "comp" group, which then might have underneath it another group called "languages", and then under that would be the actual newsgroup which would be "C". The actual newsgroup might have a name like "comp.languages.c".

Controlling Computers from a Distance

Sometimes you may want to control your computer from a remote site. And by remote site I mean somewhere other than the desk that the computer is sitting on. There are two programs that I know of that allow you to view another computer from the one that you are sitting at. One is called "PC Anywhere", and another is called "Timbuktu". You can find these programs in many computer catalogs, or you can do research for them on the Search Engines that I just mentioned. They do come in very handy, and allow you to be responsible for a network or anything else when you are away. The two previously mentioned programs are graphical and put the screen of the computer you are controlling remotely onto the monitor of the computer you are sitting at. But there is another utility program (a utility is a program that is useful in maintaining or repairing a computer. Usually they are small programs) called "telnet". This can be run from the command line (or DOS prompt as some say. It looks like this "C:" on a DOS computer, or its "MS-DOS Prompt" under Programs in the Start menu of Windows 95 or Windows 98. UNIX also has this and if you're messing with UNIX you already know what I'm talking about) of any computer that has it. This utility allows you to type in commands with the keyboard, which the remote computer will then do. You will already need a User Name and password setup for the remote computer to use telnet. If you are the Administrator of the other computer you can set this up before you need it. Otherwise have the Admin (Administrator) of the computer you want to control give you a user name and password.

Setting Up Programs to Run on a Schedule

There is another little piece of information I would like to give you. This chapter is after all, just a jumbled mix of advice that I thought might be useful. When you are running a UNIX or Windows NT network, sometimes you may want to have a program run on a regular schedule. If you went to the command line or as some people say, **DOS prompt**, and you type in the word "at" and hit the ENTER or RETURN key (same thing), you will get the brief description of the "at" command. This command will allow you to schedule just about any program or batch file (group of commands or programs in one text file) on the UNIX or Windows NT machine. But one thing I must warn you about, in Windows NT the user account that the scheduler service uses must have the authority to run the program. So just be aware of that. I'm not completely positive about the "at" command on a UNIX machine as I have never used it, but I'm told that it is usable. On UNIX there is also a command called "chron", again I can't vouch for how to use it, but look at the Man pages (It stands for Manual and is the Help system on a UNIX computer) on the UNIX computer you're running. It should give you the information you need.

Printing Getting Stuck on Windows NT

One other tidbit I'd like to enlighten you about on a Windows NT computer is the **Spooler** service. This service, which can be found under **Services** in the Windows NT control panel, controls printing. Sometimes printing will get stuck. Sometimes the only way to fix a printing problem is to stop and then restart the Spooler service. This can be done in the

Control Panel by clicking on the **Services** icon. This is just something that I have found to be useful and until recently was not documented anywhere.

Internet Service Provider (ISP)

You will need to get an Internet Service Provider (ISP) such as CompuServe, Earth Link or any number of other ISPs. You will need this ISP for electronic mail (e-mail) as well as newsgroups, etc. You probably already have one by now but if not then you need to get some way to access the Internet.

Chapter 10

A Final Word

Everything in the computer industry is continuously changing. Some say its to take advantage of the continual improvements to computer hardware, others say its so that software companies have new software to sell. Whatever the reason, it is a factor in any career in the computer industry.

By the time you read this, some of the books I recommend, some of the web sites I point you to, and maybe even some of the programming languages I talk about may not exist. But the most important thing that this book will do for you will still happen even if you read this ten years from now.

That **important** thing I mention is just to make you aware of the different possibilities for you in a computer career. While the names of certifications may change, the fact that certifications exist may be something that you were unaware of before you picked up this book. If another more modern one has replaced a programming language I mention then study that one instead. But at least now you know which one to study. Maybe you had no idea where to start before you read these few chapters, now you do.

When I first started learning about computers years ago I didn't know anything in this book. I didn't know that many computer books existed, or that I could set up a network at home, and that I could compile a program on an old computer that didn't even have a hard drive (I just used floppy disks). I learned these things through trial and error. With this book you will have a head start. I wish I knew back then what I know now. But isn't that always the way it is?

While I can't guarantee that the information contained in this book will be useful to you, I know that it sure would have been useful to me when I started out. The course of action outlined in these pages is not the easiest. It may not be the fastest, or the ideal way of breaking into a computer career. But it *can be done*. If you wanted to get to Asia and you had no money for an airplane ticket you could still walk. And when you got to the ocean you could build a raft and cross the ocean. It isn't the easiest way, or the best way, but you could still get to Asia.

Your circumstances will dictate what is the best way for you to gain the knowledge necessary for your computer career. But no matter how you get started in your career you will always need to study new information on your own. I believe this is the best way you can gain certainty on the information you read. Someone in a training class can lecture at you all they want, and maybe you can parrot back what they said to you. But do you really know the information? Are you certain it will work? When your boss asks you to do something will you feel confident that you can do it? With self-study the answer will be **yes**. Why yes? Because you've already done it yourself. You will know if it works or not.

Someone once told me that professional photographers are no different that the average person taking snapshots, it's just that they have already made all of the mistakes. It's the same with computers. Professionals are just people that have already made all the mistakes a beginner makes and so they know what will work and what will not.

So, study hard, make mistakes in the privacy of your home, and then go out and change your life.

Good Luck!

About the Author

Tom Graves is a Senior Software Consultant at a global software contracting company. He is a Software Engineer and former Microsoft Certified Systems Engineer and Network Administrator who, through self-study and the help of many knowledgeable people, learned about computers and networks.

After a successful career as a Network Administrator he went back to College and got a Master's degree in Software Engineering. Currently he is pursuing a Ph.D. in Computer Information Systems.

He lives in Southern California halfway between San Diego and Palm Springs. He is an avid fan of the Los Angeles Galaxy Soccer team and enjoys collecting coins, reading science fiction, following the Space program, traveling, and learning about people from different cultures.

He may be contacted with questions or comments at CompCareerBook@cs.com, or through the publisher.

INDEX

NOTES

NOTES

NOTES

NOTES

NOTES

NOTES

NOTES

NOTES

NOTES

NOTES

NOTES

NOTES

NOTES

NOTES

NOTES

NOTES